Nelson

ENGLISH

DEVELOPMENT

BOOK 3

JOHN JACKMAN
WENDY WREN

Nelson

Contents

Writing		Working with words
story writing – making a plan analysing writing story beginnings	filling in a planning sheet	choosing the right words
fact/opinion – which is which?	sentence writing	**snow** words
playscripts	research – dictionary	**theatre** words
magic spells descriptive	rhyming words research – dictionary	modern poetry homophones
weather report letter writing	descriptive	choosing the right words
travel brochure articles	persuasive/dissuasive	phrases to persuade/dissuade
time line letter writing	personal/autobiographical	personal details
acrostics/shape poems research – info./encyclopedia	analysing instructions making notes	similes
planning a story – endings descriptive	finishing the story lists of adjectives/adverbs	**fire** words
making notes personal – expressing preferences personal – autobiographical	descriptive	**quad**/**bi**/**tri** words
analysing types of writing classifying types of writing	purpose and audience	opposites with **dis**
imaginative – feelings	pros and cons	idioms
research ency. and info. books	interviews – note taking	writers
newspaper reports – facts	eye-witness accounts	abbreviations
purpose/audience research – thesaurus	writing for young children	complex/simple words

UNIT 1
A Winter's tale

Hunters in the Snow
by Pieter Brueghel the Elder (c. 1515–69)
Kunsthistorisches Museum, Vienna/Bridgeman Art Library, London

PICTURE STUDY

1 Write two sentences to describe what you can see in the picture.

2 Make a list of adjectives to describe:
   the people
   the landscape
   the weather.

3 If you were one of the hunters in the picture, how would you feel about being outside on such a cold day?

4

MAKING A STORY PLAN

Can you remember the things you have to think about before you write a story?

● **setting**   ● **characters**   ● **plot**

Planning your story like this helps you to sort out your ideas.
You are going to write a story about the picture *Hunters in the Snow*.

You will need to draw a planning sheet like this or ask your teacher for a photocopy of the 'story planning sheet'. Remember to leave enough space to write down your ideas.

1 Title
2 Setting
3 Characters
4 Plot   Beginning   Middle   End

Look carefully at the picture on page 4.
Fill in the planning sheet by answering these questions and jotting down some ideas.

1 **Title**
- What will you call your story? What is the **title**?
  Come back to this later if you cannot think of an interesting title at the moment.

2 **Setting**
Choose words and phrases that describe the **setting** of the picture.
- What is the weather like?
- What kind of landscape is it?

3 **Characters**
Think about the hunters, the **characters** in the story.
- What are their names?
- What do they look like?
- What kind of people are they?

4 **Plot**
You now have the setting and the characters for your story.
Think about a **plot**. What is going to happen?
- Why are the hunters there?
- What are they going to do?
- Is something going to happen to one of them?
- How is your story going to end?

If you have worked out:
where your story takes place (the **setting**)
who is in the story (the **characters**)
how your story begins, what happens, and how your story ends (the **plot**)
you can now think about other things that will make people want to read your story.

Look after your plan. You will need it after we have looked at some story beginnings.

The beginning of a story must make the reader interested enough to want to go on reading.

Look at these story beginnings:

The Weirdstone of Brisingamen by Alan Garner

The guard knocked on the door of the compartment as he went past. "Wilmslow fifteen minutes!"

"Thank you!" shouted Colin.

Susan began to clear away the debris of the journey — apple cores, orange peel, food wrappings, magazines, while Colin pulled down their luggage from the rack.

Glossary

a *glossary* explains what a word means
debris means rubbish

What we know

We know Colin and Susan are on a train. They are going to Wilmslow and will arrive in fifteen minutes.

What we don't know

Who Colin and Susan are.
Why they are going to Wilmslow.
Whether anyone will be waiting for them.

Black Beauty by Anna Sewell

The first place that I can well remember was a large pleasant meadow with a pond of clear water in it. Some shady trees leaned over it, and rushes and water lilies grew at the deep end. Over the hedge on one side we looked into a ploughed field, and on the other we looked over a gate at our master's house, which stood by the roadside; at the top of the meadow was a plantation of fir trees, and at the bottom a running brook overhung by a steep bank.

What we know
The setting for the story is the countryside.
It is the first place the storyteller can remember.

What we don't know
Who the characters are in the story.
What is going to happen.

Read these story beginnings and write about:

1 what you know

2 what you don't know.

The Enchanted Island by Ian Serraillier

Far across the sea was an enchanted island untouched by human law. In the valleys between the wooded hills there were fresh bubbling springs and fields richly fertile. The air was full of sweet sounds, of humming voices and twangling instruments that gave endless delight. In the woods filberts and crab-apples grew wild; the birds sang in the tree-tops all day long, and nimble monkeys leapt from branch to branch. The cliffs were ringed with yellow sands and sparkling seas, and the atmosphere was drowsy with enchantment.

Glossary
filberts are hazelnuts

The Secret Garden by Frances Hodgson Burnett

When Mary Lennox was sent to Misselthwaite Manor to live with her uncle, everybody said she was the most disagreeable-looking child ever seen.

The Hodgeheg by Dick King-Smith

"Your Auntie Betty has copped it," said Pa Hedgehog to Ma.

"Oh, no!" cried Ma. "Where?"

"Just down the road. Opposite the newsagent's. Bad place to cross, that."

"Everywhere's a bad place to cross nowadays," said Ma. "The traffic's dreadful."

BEGINNING YOUR OWN STORY

1 Now go back to the planning sheet you made for your story about the picture *Hunters in the Snow*.
   Think carefully about how you are going to begin.

● You could describe the setting.
● You could tell your reader about the characters.
● You could begin with a conversation.

2 Write the beginning of your story.

WORKING WITH WORDS

Choosing words carefully is important in all kinds of writing.

Look:

What you write   **What do you mean?**

                                      Snow was falling gently.

It was snowing.   It was snowing thick and fast.

                                      A snow blizzard raged outside.

Copy these word 'fans' and fill them in.

What you write   **What do you mean?**

                                      ?

It was raining.   ?

                                      ?

                                      ?

It was foggy.   ?

                                      ?

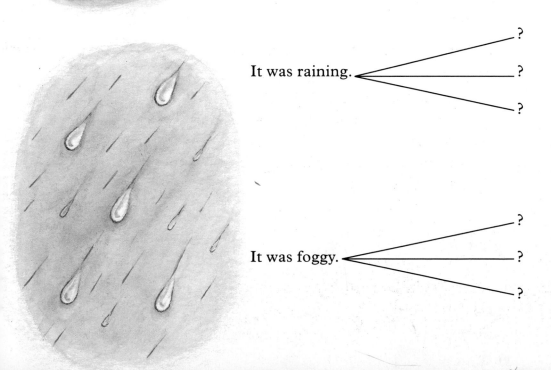

Footprints in the snow

According to the Met. Office, the winter of 1854 to 1855 was very cold, especially in the south of England. One night in February there was a heavy fall of snow in Devon and the next morning there was a line of footprints in the snow that went on for miles. They were four inches long and looked as if they had been made by something with two legs and hooves.

The footprints started in a garden in Totnes and stopped in a place called Littleham. Near a village called Dawlish the footprints went through a wood. Dogs were brought to go into the wood to see if they could catch what had made the footprints but they barked and howled and would not go in.

Many people had different opinions about what had made the footprints. Sir Richard Owen, a man who studied animals, said that they were made by a badger. Other people said it was a fox, an otter, a donkey and even a kangaroo! The Reverend Henry Fusden said the prints were made by lots of cats. The people who lived in that part of Devon had their own opinion. They were sure that the footprints were made by the devil!

Glossary
Met. Office means Meteorological Office where people study and forecast the weather
opinion means a belief or point of view

COMPREHENSION

Read the passage and answer the questions.

1 Write the phrase that tells you it had snowed a lot.

2 What did the footprints look like?

3 Why do you think the footprints were not made by an ordinary animal?

4 What do you think made the footprints?

WHAT DO WE KNOW?

Some of the things you have read about are **facts**. That means they really happened.

It is a **fact** that in the south of England the winter of 1854–5 was very cold. Another **fact** is that the weird footprints began in a garden at Totnes.

Some of the other things you have read are **opinions.** Opinions are what people believe might have happened. Look:

Some people were of the **opinion** that the footprints were made by the devil.

Here are some of the **facts** and **opinions** in *Footprints in the snow:*

Fact	Opinion
Winter 1854-5 was very cold.	Sir Richard Owen said the footprints were made by a badger.
One night in February there was a heavy fall of snow.	Some people said it was a fox, an otter, a donkey or a kangaroo.
A line of footprints went on for miles.	Reverend Henry Fusden said the prints were made by lots of cats.
Each footprint was four inches long.	The people in Devon thought that the footprints were made by the devil.

The Abominable Snowman

In every mountain range in the world there are stories of a strange man-like creature which roams around leaving huge footprints. It has many names, Yeti, Big Foot, Kang-Mi, and the one you may have heard of – the Abominable Snowman.

Whatever its name, all the descriptions are about the same. It is up to ten feet tall, weighs about 300 pounds, walks upright and is very hairy.

A British mountaineer called Eric Shipton took some photographs of human-like footprints in the Himalayas. They were 13 inches long and 8 inches wide. He said the tracks were too large to have been made by a bear. Some people think that the creature is a big ape but many do not believe it exists at all. They argue that the clues people have found, such as teeth, could be those of bears, wolves or snow leopards. It is also thought that people who claim they have seem the Abominable Snowman are just imagining things!

COMPREHENSION

Read the passage carefully.

1 Draw two columns in your book and put headings like this:

Fact   **Opinion**

_____   _____
_____   _____
_____   _____

Write any **fact** you find in your fact column.
Write any **opinion** you find in your opinion column.

2 What is your opinion of the Abominable Snowman?

3 Do you think it really exists?

WORKING WITH WORDS

These words all begin with **snow**. Copy them out and put the correct meaning next to each one:

snowball   bad weather with snow

snowdrift   a ball made of snow pressed together

snowfall   a bank of snow blown by the wind

snowline   a fall of snow

snowstorm   the level above which there is always snow

Use your dictionary to find more **snow** words.

Tudor and Stuart theatre

Watching plays has been a popular pastime since the Middle Ages. Actors performed in a churchyard or from the back of a wagon. By Tudor times theatres were being built. They were usually in the shape of a courtyard with rows of balconies for people to watch from on three sides. The balconies had a roof but the 'pit' was open to the sky. The people who stood in the pit to watch the play were called 'groundlings'.

De Witt's drawing of the Swan Theatre at Bankside from The Mansell Collection

A flag was flown from the top of the theatre and a trumpet sounded to let people know when a play was about to begin.

Boys played women's parts as it was not thought suitable for women to appear on the stage. Actors usually wore their own clothes and there was almost no scenery.

The audiences were not quiet as they are today. They would move around, play dice and buy food and drink while the play was going on. They could be very noisy indeed if they did not like the play!

Glossary
scenery means a painted backcloth for a play

THE GLOBE THEATRE IN THE DAYS OF SHAKESPEARE. GEORGE PYCROFT DEL.

COMPREHENSION

1 What problems do you think actors would have had performing from the back of a wagon?

2 Why do you think the people that watched from the pit were called 'groundlings'?

3 What sort of people do you think watched from the balconies?

4 What do you think the actors had to do when there was a lot of noise?

5 Make a list of all the differences you can find between a play in Tudor times and a play today.

A play is a story that people watch rather than read.
When it is written down it looks different from a story.
Read the beginning of the story *Hansel and Gretel*.

Hansel and Gretel

A woodcutter lived in a forest with his wife and two children.
They were very poor and could not find enough food to feed
themselves and the children. One night they sat in front of the
fire and talked about what they could do.

'We had the last loaf of bread for our supper,' said the
woodcutter.

'I know,' said his wife. 'You didn't sell any wood today.
What are we going to do?'

They looked around the house for something they could
sell but there was nothing left.

The only thing they could do was to leave the children in the
wood and hope that someone would find them and give them food.

If the story was written as a playscript it would look like this:

title —————— **Hansel and Gretel**

scene setting ————— *In the woodcutter's cottage. It is night and the children, Hansel and Gretel, are in bed.*

characters —— Woodcutter: Come over to the fire, my dear, and sit down. We must talk.

Wife: Yes, we must talk.

Woodcutter: We had the last loaf of bread for our supper.

stage directions ——— Wife: ———— (*crying*) I know. You didn't sell any wood today. What are we going to do?

dialogue Woodcutter: I don't know.

Wife: (*getting up and walking round the room*) Can we sell anything so that we can buy food?

Woodcutter: We have sold everything. There is nothing left.

Wife: We must feed the children.

Woodcutter: (*whispering*) We can't feed them. We must leave them in the wood and hope that some kind person will find them and look after them.

When you write a play you must include:

the setting – **scene**

the names of the people in the play – **characters**

what the characters say – **dialogue**

what the characters do – **stage directions**.

Tudor and Stuart beliefs

In Tudor and Stuart times people believed in witches. James I even wrote a book about them. Part of the reason for believing in witches was that there were so many things that could not be explained. Why did a seemingly healthy person suddenly die? Why did animals suddenly become sick? People in those times did not have much scientific or medical knowledge so it was easy to say that a witch had used magic spells to put a curse on someone.

If people were suspected of being witches they were put into a river or a pond. If they floated they were guilty of witchcraft and they were then burnt or hanged. If they sank they were innocent but they often died by drowning!

Between 1603 and 1683 it is believed that 70,000 people were put to death because they were found guilty of witchcraft.

Glossary

curse means a wish that something bad will happen
suspected means thought to be guilty

COMPREHENSION   Read the passage and answer the questions.

1   Why did people find it so easy to believe in witches?

2   People often blamed witches for sudden death or sickness. For what else do you think witches might have been blamed?

3   People accused of being witches were put into water to prove their guilt or innocence. Do you think this was a fair test? Give reasons for your answer.

Double, double, toil and trouble

As so many people believed in witches, it is no surprise to find them in the plays of the time.

William Shakespeare was a famous playwright and you can still see his plays performed today. One of his most famous plays is *Macbeth*. Macbeth is a Scottish lord who is told by three witches that he will become king. In one scene it is a dark and stormy night. The witches are making a magic spell and waiting for Macbeth to visit them.

A dark cave. In the middle a cauldron boiling.
Thunder. Enter the three witches.

1 Witch: Round about the cauldron go;
In the poisoned entrails throw.
Toad that under cold stone
Days and nights has thirty-one
Sweltered venom sleeping got
Boil thou first i' th' charmed pot.

All: Double, double, toil and trouble;
Fire burn, and cauldron bubble.

2 Witch: Fillet of a fenny snake,
In the cauldron boil and bake;
Eye of newt, and toe of frog,
Wool of bat, and tongue of dog,
Adder's fork, and blind-worm's sting,
Lizard's leg and howlet's wing –
For a charm of powerful trouble,
Like a hell-broth boil and bubble.

All: Double, double, toil and trouble;
Fire burn, and cauldron bubble.

2 Witch: Cool it with a baboon's blood,
Then the charm is firm and good . . .

By the pricking of my thumbs
Something wicked this way comes.
Open, locks, whoever knocks.

Enter Macbeth

The language is quite difficult but if you read carefully you should be able to:

1 Make a list of all the horrible things the witches put into the cauldron to make the magic spell.

2 Make a list of all the rhyming words.

3 Try writing your own magic spell in rhyme.

● What will your magic spell do?
● If the magic spell is to do something horrible, you might put horrible things in.
● If the magic spell is to do something good, you might put pleasant things in.

SETTING THE SCENE

All we know about the **setting** for the witches is:

'*A dark cave. In the middle a cauldron boiling. Thunder.*'

Imagine you are going to put this scene on a stage.
    Some people in your class are going to act.
    Some people are going to make the stage look like the witches' cave.
    How will it look?
Write a description of how you want the stage to look when it is set as the witches' cave.

WORKING WITH WORDS

Here is a poem about a witch. It has lots of homophones in it.

Which Witch?

Which witch wore a rough ruff,
spent days in a daze?
Which witch kept a foul fowl,
brewed a draft draught?
Which witch told a tale of a tail,
rode a hoarse horse?
Which witch flew down a flue,
tied the tide in knots?
Which witch ate eight buns,
swallowed a pair of pears?
Which witch lived in an eerie eyrie,
slew a knight at night?

I do not know which witch you mean,
I do not know which witch you've seen.
I can only pray
I'm not her prey.

John C Head

1 Choose five pairs of words that are homophones and make
   a chart like this.

Word	Meaning
rough	not smooth
ruff	starched, pleated collar worn in olden times
days	Monday, Tuesday, etc. Period of 24 hours
daze	bewildered

Use your dictionary to help you.

2 Can you find a homophone for each word?

   pair   blue   bare   stair   birth

Gale warning!

When the air moves about we say that the wind is blowing. Sometimes the air moves slowly and we get a gentle breeze. Sometimes it moves very quickly and storms and hurricanes occur.

In 1805, a British Admiral called Sir Francis Beaufort worked out what happened when the air moved at different speeds. It is very important that people have accurate information about the strength of the wind. The Beaufort Scale has been adapted for the effects of wind on the land and is still in use today.

Glossary

accurate means free from mistakes

adapt means to change something to use in another way

The Beaufort Scale

Force	Type of wind	What you can see	Speed
0	calm	smoke rises straight up	0 kph (less than 1 mph)
1	light air	smoke drifts	1–5 kph (1–3 mph)
2	light breeze	leaves rustle weathervane moves	6–11 kph (4–7 mph)
3	gentle breeze	twigs move a flag flaps	12–19 kph (8–12 mph)
4	moderate breeze	dust and paper blown down street, small branches move	20–29 kph (13–18 mph)
5	fresh breeze	small trees start to sway	30–39 kph (19–24 mph)
6	strong breeze	large branches move	40–49 kph (25–31 mph)
7	near gale	whole trees bend over	50–61 kph (32–38 mph)
8	gale	twigs break off	62–74 kph (39–46 mph)
9	strong gale	chimneys and slates crash into the street	75–88 kph (47–54 mph)
10	storm	trees uprooted buildings badly damaged	89–102 kph (55–63 mph)
11	violent storm	general destruction	103–117 kph (64–72 mph)
12	hurricane	coasts flooded devastation	over 117 kph (73 mph or more)

Glossary   *kph* means kilometres per hour   *mph* means miles per hour

COMPREHENSION   Look at the chart and answer the questions.

1 What can you see when there is a strong breeze?

2 How quickly is the wind travelling when there is a hurricane blowing?

3 What is the type of wind when you can see twigs breaking off?

4 What is the force of the wind when it is travelling at 30–39 kph?

USING THE BEAUFORT SCALE

Look at the picture.

6 pm

By using the Beaufort Scale we can write a factual report of the strength of the wind at 6 pm.

At 6 pm the weather was bright and sunny with a moderate breeze. The strength of the wind was between 20–29 kph (13–18 mph) moving small branches and blowing paper along the street.

The report contains:

the time	**6 pm**
the general weather conditions	**bright and sunny**
the strength of the wind	**moderate breeze**
the speed of the wind in kph	**20–29**
the speed of the wind in mph	**13–18**
the effects of the wind	**small branches moving, paper blown along the street**

Look at these pictures.
They show the effects of the wind at different times on one day.

7 am

11 am

3 pm

7 pm

Use what you can see in the pictures and the information on the
Beaufort Scale to write a factual report on the general weather
conditions and the wind at different times of the day. The first
one is done for you:

At 7 am there was a light breeze. This was force 2, travelling
at 6–11 kph, and the leaves on the trees were rustling.

DESCRIPTIVE WRITING

We could write about the four pictures in a different way for a different purpose.

Imagine you are writing a letter to a friend or relative describing the day when the wind was very strong.

What you might put in your letter:

how you felt about what was happening

if you stayed indoors or had to go out

if you had to change your plans

the effects of the wind on the things around where you live.

What you wouldn't put in your letter:

the speed of the wind in kph or mph

the name of the strength of the wind.

Set out your letter remembering your address and how you finish a letter to someone you know.

WORKING WITH WORDS

1 Another word 'fan'.

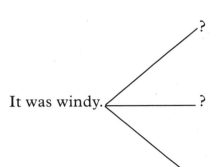

If you write 'It was windy' it doesn't give your reader much information.
What could you write to describe the wind in more detail?

It was windy.

? ? ?

2 These words describe types of wind.
Look the words up in a dictionary and write a description of each one.

hurricane

breeze

gale

typhoon

tempest

mistral

tornado

India

Russia

China

Afghanistan

Pakistan

Nepal

Bhutan

Bangla-desh

Using an encyclopedia

If we want to find out factual information about something, one of the most useful places to look is an encyclopedia.

This is what The Macmillan Encyclopedia tells us about India.

INDIA

India, Republic of (Hindi name: Bharat) A country in southern Asia; the seventh largest in the world. Its population is the seventh largest in the world. It borders on Pakistan, China, Nepal, Bhutan, Bangladesh and Burma. About 1600 languages and dialects are spoken. The main religions are Hinduism and Islam. The main food crops are rice, pulses and cereals. Tea, jute, cotton and tobacco are also important. Coal is mined and oil is produced from the Arabian Sea. India has industries such as steel, chemicals, electronics and silk textiles.

ARABIAN SEA

BAY OF BENGAL

SCALE

0   100   200   300

MILES

N W E S

INDIAN OCEAN

Sri Lanka

COMPREHENSION

To make sure you have understood what the encyclopedia has told you about India you need to:

1 Look at a map and find the places that are on India's borders.

2 Use a dictionary to find the meanings of words you do not understand. Some of the words you might look up are:

population
dialects
pulses
jute
industries

Now answer these questions.

1 What is the Hindi name for India?

2 What is a dialect?

3 What are India's main food crops?

4 Is the Arabian Sea to the north, south, east or west of India?

5 Can you find out the names of two cereal crops grown in India?

WRITING TO PERSUADE

If you were going to visit India you could look in an encyclopedia to find out some facts about the country. You could also look at travel books and brochures to find out what you could see there.

People who write travel brochures are trying to **persuade** you to visit. They don't write a long list of facts. They write descriptions that are exciting and that make you want to go and see for yourself.

1   This is how one travel brochure persuades you to visit India:

India will set your pulse racing. It's exciting, it's exotic. India is a riot of colour, a clamour of noise – things happen all the time.

You will see the temples and palaces of the fabulously rich and the grinding poverty of the less fortunate. This is India – you'll see the Taj Mahal at sunset, ride on the back of an elephant to the Amber Fort, taste food as varied as the country itself. You will be thrilled, fascinated, maybe occasionally shocked – but never bored. We will show you markets and bazaars where you can bargain for silks and spices, silver and rubies, carpets and crisp cottons. And you'll leave India vowing to return!

2 Another travel brochure persuades you to visit India's beaches:

Beaches so clean a turtle could eat his dinner off them. Glass clear seas where the only oil pollution comes from the occasional coconut that rolls into the surf. Beaches of beautiful white coral sand that stretch for miles, backed by thickets of shady palm.

Look again at what the encyclopedia has to say about India and then read the travel brochures. The language they use is very different.

3 Make a list of words and phrases in the travel brochures that would make you want to visit India. Think about:

- what you would see
- how you would feel
- what you could do.

33

Visit the Taj Mahal

This is what you would find out about the Taj Mahal in an encyclopedia:

> The Taj Mahal is a tomb in Agra in Northern India. It is
> surrounded by gardens. It is built mainly of white marble with
> lots of carvings and precious stones. The emperor Shah Jahan
> built it in memory of his wife Mumtaz Mahal who died in 1631.

1 You are writing in a travel brochure to persuade people
   to visit the Taj Mahal. Think carefully about the language you
   would use to show people that is it something they really should
   go and see.

2 Write about the place where you live or about your school to
   persuade a friend to come and visit.

WRITING TO DISSUADE

When you are trying to **persuade** someone to go somewhere you use words to show them how pleasant and exciting the visit will be.

If you are trying to persuade someone NOT to go, you use words to show them how unpleasant and awful the visit will be. You try to **dissuade** them.

Write about one of the following to **dissuade** a friend from going to visit:

the circus

the swimming baths

the park.

WORKING WITH WORDS

When you are writing to **persuade** or **dissuade** someone about something you need to choose words carefully.

If you wanted to persuade someone to eat a meal, would you say that it **tastes good** or that it is **really delicious**?

If you wanted to persuade someone to come to the pictures with you, would you say that the film is **okay** or that it is **very exciting**?

1   Look at the list of phrases. Write some sentences to describe them in a way that would **persuade** people to buy them?

a good book

a pretty dress

a nice cake

a friendly dog

a little model car

GUFFAW COMIC

a funny story

2   Now write some sentences that would **dissuade** people from buying them.

An Indian childhood

Autobiographies

The word **autobiography** comes from three Greek words:

auto = self   *bios* = life   *graphos* = writing

It is a story written by someone about his/her own life.

Here is a story written by Madhur Jaffrey about her childhood in India.

The days of the banyan tree

There was an old banyan tree that grew just outside our house. It was more than a tree, it seemed to be a whole forest, all by itself.

Its trunk went up, up, and up, almost a hundred feet. Some of the branches, instead of rising and spreading like outstretched arms, made nosedives towards the earth, where they burrowed in, took root, and reappeared as fresh trunks. My nanny – or *aya*, as we called her – said that the roots of a banyan tree went all the way to the Underworld and that when they rose again as fresh trunks, they carried up with them all sorts of ghosts and goblins. She insisted that there never was a banyan tree without a few ghosts lurking in its branches.

I believed her.

My grandmother, on the other hand, said that the banyan tree was a blessed tree because it had the wisdom of its years and because it provided so much shade. In fact, in the burning months of May and June, we prayed to it and offered it the best of the summer's yield – seedless cucumbers, watermelons, aubergines and mangoes.

I saw my grandmother's point. In the summer, scorching winds blasted in from neighbouring deserts carrying with them particles of sand to irritate eyes and parch throats. When the sky overhead felt like an oven with its door left open by some careless cook, the banyan trees offered cool, natural arbours to perspiring travellers.

My grandmother always advised me, 'On your way back from school, remember to get off your bicycle and rest under the shade of the banyan tree.'

Rest under the banyan tree and bump into a ghost!

Oh dear me, no! I paid no attention to my grandmother. In fact, when I reached the banyan trees, I held my breath and bicycled for my life.

No ghosts were going to catch me!

Madhur Jaffrey

Glossary

nanny or *aya* is someone trained to look after children

COMPREHENSION   Read the passage and answer the questions.

1   Why did the banyan tree seem to be 'a whole forest, all by itself'?

2   What is the Underworld?

3   Write the words and phrases that tell you it is much hotter in India than it is here.

4   Why did the writer ignore her grandmother's advice?

37

Bushfire

Five children are caught up in a bushfire that sweeps across dry grassland. They are searching for a friend called Shane. Jan set out alone, and is separated from the others. Suddenly they find that they are trapped and in danger of being caught by the fire.

They plunged on. Sometimes they were engulfed in clouds of smoke like stinking yellow mountain mist, but Bill knew the way so well that he went forward unerringly.

Suddenly he stopped. 'Listen! A coo-ee!'

The long-drawn-out first syllable floated to them on the smoke, followed by the whip-like ending.

'Jan?'

Jan was coo-eeing. It did not sound very loud; there were too many other noises to drown the call.

They listened. Each coo-ee came nearer. It was unlikely that she thought they would be on this track; probably she wanted anyone at all who might be in this vicinity to know she was there.

'She's coming back – coming this way!'

Then Jan came out of the smoke. She was crying, and so distraught that she didn't ask how or why they were there. Perhaps she understood. Shane was their friend, too.

'Fire's right across the track! We can't get through!'

'How near?'

'Quarter of a mile, p'raps. Not burning as fast now. But creeping up over everything, swallowing everything. . .

'I can't get through. I can't get through to Shane!' Jan was streaked with grime and smoke and tears. . .

Now they realised that the wind was not altogether subdued by the cold front. That a fierce gust had arisen again, and fire was spotting over their heads. Fire-brands were lobbing behind them. A series of missiles, as though the fire had suddenly found its mark, and was aiming with accuracy. It would veer again but not before its mischief had been done. It had all the viciousness of fire out of control . . . of wildfire.

Bill knew, and the others were scarcely less quick to realise, that retreat was cut off.

from 'Wildfire' by *Mavis Thorpe Clark*

Glossary

engulfed means swallowed up

vicinity means nearby

distraught means upset

p'raps means perhaps

subdued means calmed

fire-brands are burning pieces of wood

retreat is the way back

COMPREHENSION   True or false?

1   Bill was unsure of the way to go.

2   Jan's call was not very loud.

3   She was calling because she knew that her friends were on the track.

4   The wind was blowing the fire towards them.

5   The only way to safety was to go back.

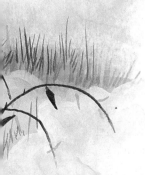

STORY ENDINGS   Read the passage again and think how you might end the story. The kind of ending you write will depend on how you want your reader to feel.

1 **Happy ever after**   The children quickly find a way out of the fire. A storm blows up and the rain puts the fire out. No one is hurt.

2 **Fear and excitement**   The children find it very difficult to escape. They try one way and then another and they are always cut off by the fire. Just when there seems to be no hope, they are rescued and taken to safety.

3 Sadness

The children eventually escape from the fire but one of them is hurt badly on the way.

4 Unexpectedly surprised

The children are trapped and there is no way out.
A spacecraft lands from another planet and rescues them.

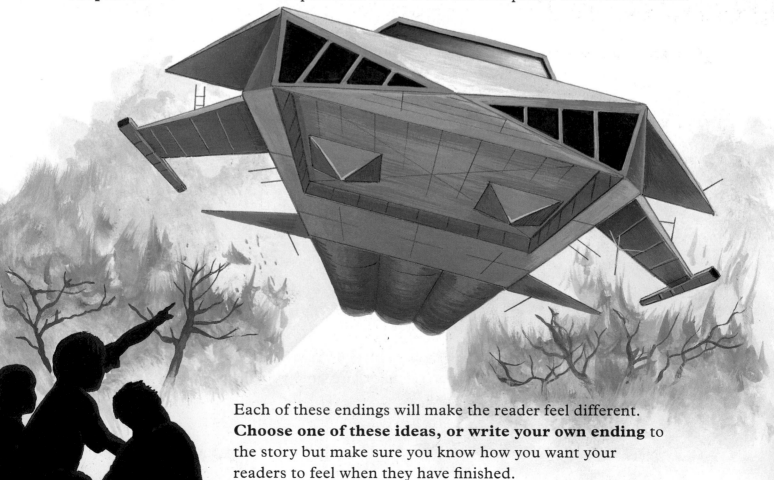

Each of these endings will make the reader feel different.
Choose one of these ideas, or write your own ending to the story but make sure you know how you want your readers to feel when they have finished.

The painting shows a bushfire in Africa.
You could describe this quite simply by saying:

Hunters and animals are caught in a big fire.

This is what the picture is about but the sentence does not tell
you very much.

To describe the picture properly you need to think about the words you can use to describe what you can see and also what you think the animals and the hunters are feeling.

Look at the fire.

1 Make a list of words that describe its colour and size.
- How is the fire burning?
- Is it gentle?
- Is it raging out of control?

Look at the animals.

2 Make a list of words to describe how they are moving.
- Are they strolling about?
- Are they leaping wildly?

Look at the hunters.

3 Make a list of words to describe how you think they are feeling.
- Are they calm and untroubled?
- Are they panicking and alarmed?

4 Now write your description of the picture.

WORKING WITH WORDS

Put each of these **fire** words into a sentence.
Use a dictionary to help you.

fire-alarm

fire-fighter

fire-brand

fire-brigade

fire-escape

fire-eater

Victorian schooldays

Cambo schoolroom, Northumberland. The teacher, Miss Ellen Richardson, shown with the pupil teacher, having charge over some 70 children. The walls are covered with display charts. Date of photograph c. 1890.

COMPREHENSION

Look carefully at the photographs.
One shows you a classroom in Victorian times.
The other shows a classroom today.

1   Make a list of all the things which are different
    and a list of any things which are the same.
    Look at:

● the things in the classroom

● the way the pupils and teachers are dressed

● how the classroom is arranged.

Use your lists to write:

2   a description of a Victorian classroom

3   a description of a modern classroom

4   which one you like best and why you like it.

Imagine you have been asked to build the perfect classroom.

5   Make a list of all the things you think should be in it.

6   Make a list of the things you think should definitely **not**
    be in it.

Hard Times

Mr Thomas Gradgrind is a teacher in Charles Dickens's book 'Hard Times'. He is not interested in what the children think or feel. He is only interested in facts!

'Girl number twenty,' said Mr Gradgrind, squarely pointing with his square forefinger, 'I don't know that girl. Who is that girl?'

'Sissy Jupe, sir,' explained number twenty, blushing, standing up, and curtseying.

'Sissy is not a name,' said Mr Gradgrind. 'Don't call yourself Sissy. Call yourself Cecilia.'

'It's father as calls me Sissy, sir,' returned the young girl in a trembling voice, and with another curtsey.

'Then he has no business to do it,' said Mr Gradgrind. 'Tell him he mustn't. Cecilia Jupe. Let me see. What is your father?'

'He belongs to the horse-riding, if you please, sir.'

Mr Gradgrind frowned, and waved off the objectionable calling with his hand.

'We don't want to know anything about that, here. You mustn't tell us about that, here. Your father breaks horses, don't he?'

'If you please, sir, when they can get any to break, they do break horses in the ring, sir . . .'

'Very well, then . . . Give me your definition of a horse.'

(Sissy Jupe thrown into the greatest alarm by this demand.)

'Girl number twenty unable to define a horse!' said Mr Gradgrind . . . 'Girl number twenty possessed of no facts, in reference to one of the commonest of animals! Some boy's definition of a horse. Bitzer, yours. . . .'

'Quadruped. Graminivorous. Forty teeth, namely twenty-four grinders, four eye-teeth, and twelve incisive. Sheds coat in the spring; in marshy countries, sheds hoofs, too. Hoofs hard, but requiring to be shod with iron. Age known by marks in mouth.'

'Now girl number twenty,' said Mr Gradgrind. 'You know what a horse is.'

Charles Dickens

Glossary

objectionable means not liked
calling means job or profession
breaks means tames
definition means meaning

quadruped means four-footed animal
graminivorous mean grass-eating
grinders means teeth

COMPREHENSION

1 Write down the reasons why you would or would not like Mr Gradgrind as a teacher.

2 What does the fact that Sissy was known as 'girl number twenty' tell you about the kind of school it was?

3 Do you think Bitzer's description of a horse is a good one?

4 If you were asked to describe a horse, what would you say?

5 Do you think Mr Gradgrind is right about only wanting to know facts?

WRITING ABOUT YOUR OWN EXPERIENCE

Sissy Jupe met Mr Gradgrind on her first day at school.
Can you remember your first day at school?
Write about what you can remember. The drawings will help you.

What I felt like.

my first teacher

the other boys and girls

What I did on my first day in the classroom.

playtime

lunch time

Did I want to go back the next day?

WORKING WITH WORDS

1 Bitzer describes a horse as a **quadruped** which means that it has four feet.

quad means four

Use a dictionary to find one meaning for each **quad** word:

quadrangle

quadrilateral

quadrille

Can you find any more quad words?

2 A **bicycle** has two wheels.

bi means two

Use a dictionary to find the meanings of these **bi** words:

biped

bifocal

bilingual

3 A **triangle** has three sides.

tri means three

Use a dictionary to find the meanings of these **tri** words:

tricycle

trio

triplets

4 Find as many **bi** words and **tri** words as you can.

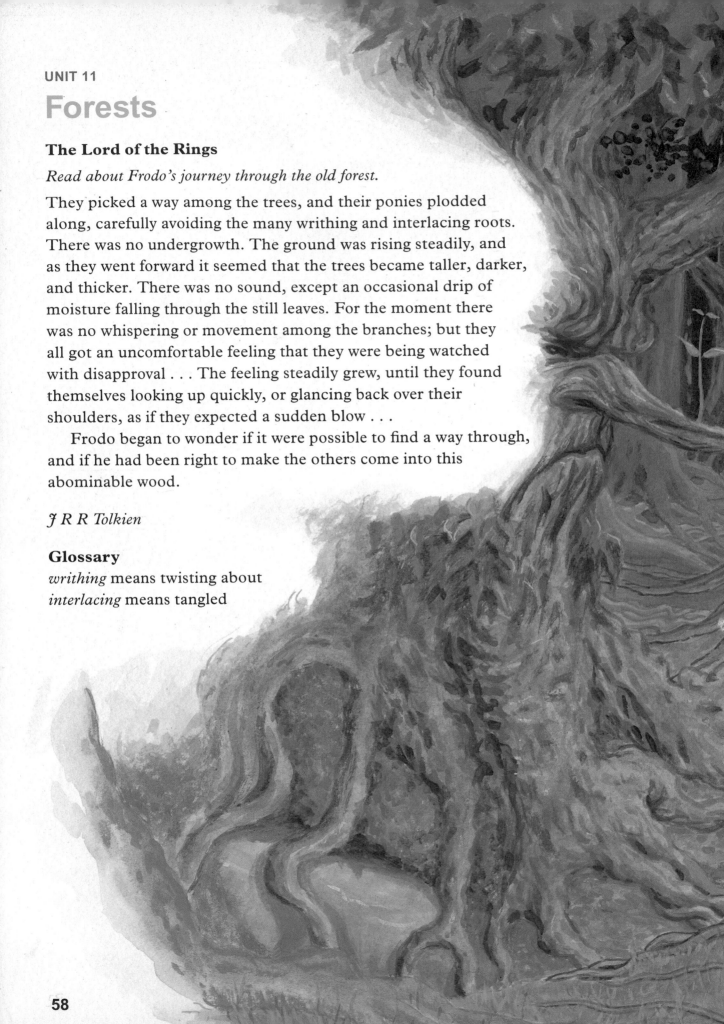

Forests

The Lord of the Rings

Read about Frodo's journey through the old forest.

They picked a way among the trees, and their ponies plodded along, carefully avoiding the many writhing and interlacing roots. There was no undergrowth. The ground was rising steadily, and as they went forward it seemed that the trees became taller, darker, and thicker. There was no sound, except an occasional drip of moisture falling through the still leaves. For the moment there was no whispering or movement among the branches; but they all got an uncomfortable feeling that they were being watched with disapproval . . . The feeling steadily grew, until they found themselves looking up quickly, or glancing back over their shoulders, as if they expected a sudden blow . . .

Frodo began to wonder if it were possible to find a way through, and if he had been right to make the others come into this abominable wood.

J R R Tolkien

Glossary
writhing means twisting about
interlacing means tangled

COMPREHENSION

Read the passage and answer the questions.

1 Write the words and phrases that the writer uses to describe the forest.

2 How does the description of the forest make you feel?

3 Do you think Frodo and his friends enjoy the ride through the forest?

4 Why does the writer call it an 'abominable wood'?

5 Find the words in the passage that mean the same as:

– keeping away from

– happening now and then

– speaking in a soft, low voice.

Learning about forests

Look at the diagram and notes on the forest.

1. The top layer of the forest is called the **canopy**. The leaves of the tallest trees push their way into the sunlight. They need the energy from the sun to grow.

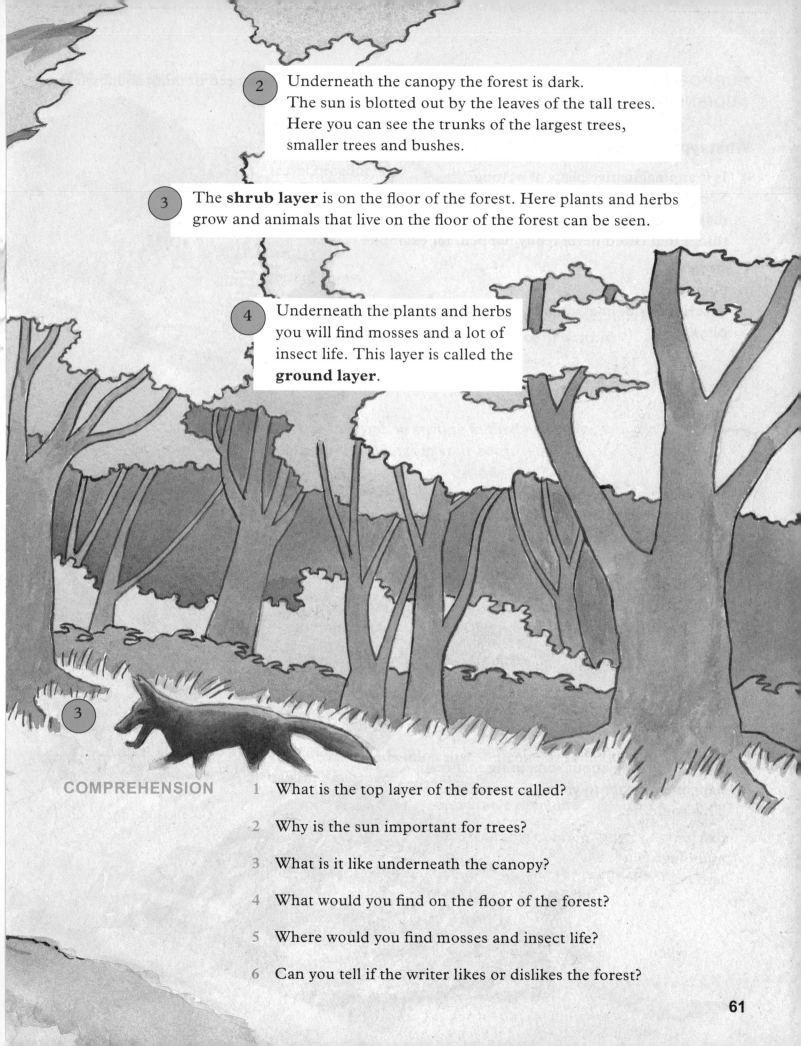

2 Underneath the canopy the forest is dark.
The sun is blotted out by the leaves of the tall trees.
Here you can see the trunks of the largest trees,
smaller trees and bushes.

3 The **shrub layer** is on the floor of the forest. Here plants and herbs grow and animals that live on the floor of the forest can be seen.

4 Underneath the plants and herbs you will find mosses and a lot of insect life. This layer is called the **ground layer**.

COMPREHENSION

1 What is the top layer of the forest called?

2 Why is the sun important for trees?

3 What is it like underneath the canopy?

4 What would you find on the floor of the forest?

5 Where would you find mosses and insect life?

6 Can you tell if the writer likes or dislikes the forest?

61

Eat to live

All living things need food.
Carnivores are meat eaters.
Herbivores are plant eaters.
Omnivores eat meat and plants.

Today most people buy their food from shops.
Long ago people had to grow their own food and hunt animals to live.
Today people still hunt but it is usually not for food but as a sport.

Reynard the Fox

*This is part of a poem by John Masefield about a fox
who is being hunted by men and dogs.*

The fox was strong, he was full of running,
He could run for an hour and then be cunning,
But the cry behind him made him chill,
They were nearer now and they meant to kill.
They meant to run him until his blood
Clogged on his heart as his brush with mud,
Till his back bent up and his tongue hung flagging,
And his belly and brush were filthed with dragging.
Till he crouched stone-still, dead-beat and dirty,
With nothing but teeth against the thirty.
And all the way to that blinding end
He would meet with men and have none his friend:
Men to holloa and men to run him,
With stones to stagger and yells to stun him;
Men to head him, with whips to beat him,
Teeth to mangle, and mouths to eat him.
And all the way, that wild high crying
To cold his blood with the thought of dying,
The horn and the cheer, and the drum-like thunder
Of the horsehooves stamping the meadows under.
He upped his brush and went with a will
For the Sarsen Stones on Wan Dyke Hill.

John Masefield

Glossary
brush means fox's tail
holloa means to shout

Read the poem and answer the questions.

1 The fox was good at doing certain things that would help him to survive. What were they?

2 What sort of people do you think the men were who were chasing the fox?

3 What will the fox feel like if he is caught?

4 What does the expression 'went with a will' mean?

5 Does the poet want you to be on the side of the fox or of the men? How can you tell?

WRITING ABOUT FEELINGS

When we write stories and poems we write about what characters do and say. We also need to consider what they **think** and **feel** to help the reader understand what sort of characters they are.

Imagine you are Reynard and you are chased by a pack of dogs and men on horses. You reach the safety of your den and you are telling the other foxes about the chase.

Remember to include:

● where you were and what you were doing before the chase began

● when you realised the dogs and men were nearby

● how you felt while you were being chased

● how you managed to escape

● how you felt when you reached home safely.

I Saw a Jolly Hunter

I saw a jolly hunter
   With a jolly gun
Walking in the country
   In the jolly sun.

In the jolly meadow
   Sat a jolly hare.
Saw the jolly hunter.
   Took jolly care.

Hunter jolly eager –
   Sight of jolly prey.
Forgot gun pointing
   Wrong jolly way.

Jolly hunter jolly head
   Over heels gone.
Jolly old safety-catch
   Not jolly on.

Bang went the jolly gun.
   Hunter jolly dead.
Jolly hare got clean away,
   Jolly good, I said.

Charles Causley

COMPREHENSION

Read the poem and answer the questions.

1 The **theme** of a piece of writing is the main subject that the writing is about.
    Reynard the Fox and *I Saw a Jolly Hunter* have the same **theme**. What is it?

2 Do you think both poets feel the same about their theme?

3 How do they feel?

4 How do they want you to feel?

WRITING TO PERSUADE

There are many things that happen in our daily lives that we feel strongly about.

We may be **for** them or **against** them, for instance:

you may feel strongly that you should not have to wear school uniform – you would be **against** wearing uniform

you may feel strongly that smoking should be banned – you would be **for** a ban on smoking.

If you simply said, 'I am against wearing school uniform,' somebody would probably say, 'Why?'

If you simply said, 'I support a ban on smoking,' somebody would probably say, 'Why?'

To persuade people that they should agree with your side of an argument you need to think of reasons to convince them.

1   Think about fox hunting.
    Write two headings in your book:

    For   **Against**

    Now write down all the reasons you can think of for agreeing with fox hunting as a sport and all the reasons for being against it.

2   Do the same for one of these:
    wearing school uniform
    smoking
    something else you feel strongly about.

WORKING WITH WORDS

These expressions are called idioms.

Did you find out the meaning of the expression 'went with a will'? There are lots of expressions in English that look odd but most people will know what they mean.

Try to find out what people mean when they say:

once in a blue moon

stick to your guns

a bolt from the blue

over the moon.

DANGER AT SEA

The Times reported what it was like at sea during the gale:

'The Sealink ferry, *Hengist*, was blown aground close to Folkstone harbour, but it was carrying no passengers and the crew of 22 were rescued by breeches-buoy.'

' "The seas were murderous. We could hardly see anything, with huge waves, a wall of spray and the lashing wind," said a coastguard spokesman.'

Photographer: Paul Amos

WRITING A NEWSPAPER REPORT

The words, map and the picture give you lots of information about what it must have been like during the storm.

The whole report gives you the **facts** such as the strength of the wind and the various things that happened.

It also gives you an idea of what people thought about the storm. The coastguard was actually there and what he said is known as an **eye-witness account**.

1   Imagine you are a newspaper reporter writing your report the day after the storm. You can use any of the **facts** you like from *The Times* but you have to make up two **eye-witness accounts**.

Here are some suggestions of people you might interview:
  – a fire-fighter who rescued someone from a falling building
  – a driver whose car was stuck in a minor road
  – crew member of the Hengist ferry who was rescued
  – a home owner whose roof was blown off.

2   If you can, think of other people who would have been affected by the storm whom you could interview.

3   When you have written your newspaper report, give it a title.

WORKING WITH WORDS

The Meteorological Office is where people study and forecast the weather.
It is called the Met. Office for short.
When we shorten a name we call it an **abbreviation**.
Usually there is a list of abbreviations in the back of a dictionary.
What are these abbreviations for?

adj	cert	Dr	GB
cm	MP	RSPCA	Ave

Earth . . . In the beginning

Nearly every culture has ancient stories about how the earth came into being. These stories were told to satisfy people's curiosity about the planet they lived on. The stories usually have a powerful god who was the creator.

Read these two versions of the creation of the earth:

The Bible

In the beginning everything was dark. There was no world at all, only emptiness, but God was there and he was not dark or empty.

God said, 'Let there be light!' And there was light. Now life could begin.

So God shaped the world; he made the sky, the land and the sea. The earth was hot. Fire rumbled in the heart of the mountains. They exploded. Then, slowly, the earth cooled, leaving rich soil where plants could grow. God was pleased with the world he had made.

Now he wanted plants to grow on the earth. Green shoots sprang up, and flowers opened their gay petals. Grass spread over the hills and valleys and a gentle wind rustled the leaves of countless trees. God saw that it was all good.

The green shoots grew tall and yellow. Grain ripened in the sun, but no little harvest mice ran through the corn. No birds nested in the tall trees. No children played yet in the new world.

So God spoke to the sea and the sky, 'Be filled with living things, too!' Fish of every shape and colour filled the sea. In the sky above, birds flew, soaring high as they sang. Insects hovered over the earth. Then God said, 'Let the earth be filled with animals of every kind!' Large animals roamed over the earth, and small ones scuttled after them. The air was filled with roars, neighs and squeals. God blessed them. Their numbers grew. God was pleased with everything he had made.

Now the earth was ready for people to live on it. God took a handful of soil and made a man. He breathed his life-giving breath into him. The man was different from all the other animals God made.

Jenny Robertson

77

The Egyptian story of creation

In the beginning, before there was any land Of Egypt, all was darkness, and there was nothing but a great waste of water called Nu. The power of Nu was such that there rose out of the darkness a great shining egg, and this was Ra.

Now Ra was all powerful, and he could take many forms. His power and the secret of it lay in his hidden name; but if he spoke other names, that which he named came into being. 'I am Khepera at the dawn, and Ra at noon and Tum in the evening,' he said. And the sun rose and passed across the sky, and set for the first time.

Then he named Shu, and the first winds blew; he named Refnut the spitter and the first rain fell. Next he named Geb, and the earth came into being; he named the goddess Nut, and she was the sky arched over the earth with her feet on one horizon and her hands on the other; he named Hapi, and the great river Nile flowed through Egypt and made it fruitful.

After this Ra named all things that are upon the earth, and they grew. Last of all he named mankind, and there were men and women in the land of Egypt.

Then Ra took on the shape of a man and became the first Pharaoh, ruling over the whole country for thousands and thousands of years, and giving such harvests that for ever afterwards the Egyptians spoke of the good things 'which happened in the time of Ra'.

78

COMPREHENSION

In many ways the Bible story of creation and the Egyptian story of creation are similar; in many ways they are different.

To decide how they are similar and how they are different answer the following questions:

1   Who was responsible for the creation in both stories. How were they different?

2   How did the creators make things?

3   Make a list of everything created in the Bible story and the order in which they were created.

4   Make a list of everything created in the Egyptian story and the order in which they were created.

5   Look at your lists. Are there any similarities? Are there any differences?

PRESENTING INFORMATION

The two accounts of creation that you have read are presented as written stories which we call **continuous prose**.

There are many other ways of presenting these stories which will make them suitable for a different audience.

1   Imagine you are writing one of the creation stories as a book for a young child who is just learning to read.
    You will need to consider:

●   the type of words you use - you will have to use simple language

●   repetition of words

●   how you will divide up the story - what will go on each page

●   how many words on a page

●   pictures to help the child understand what is happening

2   Plan your book carefully:

●   How many pages will you need?

●   What title will you give your book?

●   Will each page have a picture?

When you have divided up the story and planned the book, look at **Working with words** to help you make the words simpler, and then go ahead and make your book.

He made the sky, the land, the sea

WORKING WITH WORDS

Using a **thesaurus** can help you find simpler words for your story.

For 'hover' you could use 'fly'.

For 'countless' you could use 'lots'.

Look up these words in your thesaurus and find simpler ones with the same meaning:

roam   explode   soar